The 16-Point Strategy for Productivity and Total Quality

The Management Master Series

William F. Christopher
Editor-in-Chief

7

The 16-Point
Strategy for
Productivity and
Total Quality

William F. Christopher
and
Carl G. Thor

PRODUCTIVITY PRESS

Portland, Oregon

Volume 7 of the *Management Master Series*
William F. Christopher, Editor-in-Chief
Copyright © 1995 by Productivity Press, Inc.

Productivity Press
P.O. Box 13390
Portland, OR 97213-0390
United States of America
Telephone: 503-235-0600
Telefax: 503-235-0909

ISBN: 1-56327-072-2

Book and cover design by William Stanton
Cover illustration by Paul Zwolak
Typeset by Laser Words, Madras, India
Printed and bound by BookCrafters in the United States of America

Library of Congress Cataloging-in-Publication Data

Christopher, William F.
    The 16-point strategy for productivity and total quality / William F. Christopher and Carl G. Thor.
        p.   cm. – (Management master series; v. 7)
    1. Industrial management. 2. Industrial productivity. 3. Quality control. I. Thor, Carl G. II. Title. III. Title: The sixteen-point strategy for productivity and total quality. IV. Series.
    HD31.C524   1995   94-23997
    658.5–dc20   CIP

00 99 98 97 96 95   10 9 8 7 6 5 4 3 2 1

—CONTENTS—

PUBLISHER'S MESSAGE

The *Management Master Series* was designed to discover and disseminate to you the world's best concepts, principles, and current practices in excellent management. We present this information in a concise and easy-to-use format to provide you with the tools and techniques you need to stay abreast of this rapidly accelerating world of ideas.

World-class competitiveness requires managers today to be thoroughly informed about how and what other internationally successful managers are doing. What works? What doesn't? and Why?

Management is often considered a "neglected art." It is not possible to know how to manage before you are made a manager. But once you become a manager you are expected to know how to manage and to do it well, right from the start.

One result of this neglect in management training has been managers who rely on control rather than creativity. Certainly, managers in this century have shown a distinct neglect of workers as creative human beings. The idea that employees are an organization's most valuable asset is still very new. How managers can inspire and direct the creativity and intelligence of everyone involved in the work of an organization has only begun to emerge.

Perhaps if we consider management as a "science" the task of learning how to manage well will be easier. A scientist begins with an hypothesis and then runs experiments to observe whether the hypothesis is correct. Scientists depend on detailed notes about the experiment—the timing, the ingredients, the amounts—and carefully record all results as they test new hypotheses. Certain things come to be known by this method; for instance, that water always consists of one part oxygen and two parts hydrogen.

We as managers must learn from our experience and from the experience of others. The scientific approach provides a model for learning. Science begins with vision and desired outcomes, and achieves its purpose through observation, experiment, and analysis of precisely recorded results. And then what is newly discovered is shared so that each person's research will build on the work of others.

Our organizations, however, rarely provide the time for learning or experimentation. As a manager, you need information from those who have already experimented and learned and recorded their results. You need it in brief, clear, and detailed form so that you can apply it immediately.

It is our purpose to help you confront the difficult task of managing in these turbulent times. As the shape of leadership changes, The *Management Master Series* will continue to bring you the best learning available to support your own increasing artistry in the evolving science of management.

We at Productivity Press are grateful to William F. Christopher and our staff of editors who have searched out those masters with the knowledge, experience, and ability to write concisely and completely on excellence in management practice. We wish also to thank the individual volume authors; Diane Asay, project manager; Julie Zinkus, manuscript editor; Karen Jones, managing editor; Bill Stanton, design and production management; Susan Swanson, production coordination; Laser Words, text and graphics composition.

Norman Bodek
Publisher

THE 16-POINT STRATEGY FOR PRODUCTIVITY AND TOTAL QUALITY

1. **Vision.** Create a Vision and structure operations to make it happen.

2. **Goal.** Make improving Total Productivity a key goal of management at all levels.

3. **Customers.** Focus productivity improvement on creating customers and satisfying their expectations.

4. **Outcomes.** Include in productivity measures the longer-term outcomes of all company actions.

5. **Measures.** Have everyone develop specific performance measures and related goals.

6. **Empowerment.** Empower people. Put responsibility and authority where the work is done.

7. **Teamwork.** Teamwork works! Develop teams at all levels.

8. **Continuous Improvement.** Continuously improve work processes. Find and eliminate waste. Simplify and standardize. Use visual controls and mistakeproofing devices.

9. **Excellence.** Find best practices. Benchmark key business processes. Set goals to equal or exceed. Strive for excellence.

10. **Innovation.** Innovate! Encourage creativity. Search for and adopt new technology. Change and improve products, processes, information systems, communications, organization structure, and methods.

11. **Management Focus.** Create a work structure that produces the desired results. Support people.

12. **Learning.** Create a learning organization. Make ongoing education and enriching work experience part of the job.

13. **Systems.** Use systems thinking and system models to aid decisions at all levels.

14. **Celebration.** Recognize, celebrate, and reward productivity improvement.

15. **Sharing.** Share your experience. Help government and community organizations improve productivity, too.

16. **Change.** Embrace change! Use these 16 Points and keep improving!

INTRODUCTION

Marcel Proust, the French novelist, once wrote: "The real voyage of discovery consists not in seeking new lands, but in seeing with new eyes." Much that's in these 16 Points requires a reframing of traditional thought. Most of the elements seem familiar, but with these 16 points they are seen with new eyes. They're seen and understood differently, and acted on with different results.

A good definition of productivity helps us see more clearly the value of improving productivity. We can begin with the basic formula:

$$\text{Productivity (P)} = \frac{\text{Output (O)}}{\text{Input (I)}}$$

To understand productivity measures, we need definitions for both output and input that are practical and useful for today's environment of world-class competition:

Output is product or service that is delivered to customers and satisfies their needs and expectations. Company output is not measured at the end of the production line; it's measured at the end of the delivery line. Output is output to customers.

Input is the resources used to produce the output, including labor, capital, materials, energy, and other purchases.

Specifying these inputs, the productivity formula becomes:

$$P = \frac{O}{L + K + M + E + OP}$$

where   P = productivity
        O = output, as defined above
        L = labor input
        K = capital input
        M = materials input
        E = energy input
       OP = other purchases

For purposes of calculation, in most cases these input values are expressed in constant dollars. Partial productivity measures can be calculated for each of the inputs.

With this formula and these definitions, an overall measure of quality is included in the measure of productivity. Both quality and productivity aim for the same goal: to produce and deliver without error and without waste the products and services that customers need and expect.

A single calculation using the formula is not useful in itself. What matters are the change and trend in this measure over time. And the objective is constant and continuous improvement at all levels:

Levels	Benefits
National	Economic growth and elimination of government deficits
Industry	Lower costs and prices
Company	Profitability and survival
Personal	Self-fulfillment and income

At the personal level, productivity improvement is the major source for increases in real personal income. Figure 1 shows this relationship over the 39 years from 1950 to 1989.

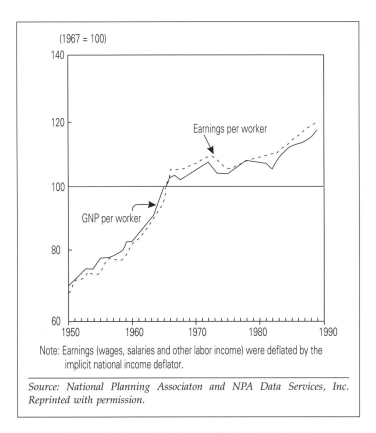

Note: Earnings (wages, salaries and other labor income) were deflated by the implicit national income deflator.

Source: National Planning Associaton and NPA Data Services, Inc. Reprinted with permission.

Figure 1. GNP per Worker and Earnings per Worker, 1950–1989

Since the late 1960s, productivity improvement in the United States has slowed. If we can increase productivity to earlier levels or better, we can achieve economic growth for our country, eliminate government deficits, lower costs and prices, sustain growth and profitability for our companies, and provide self-fulfillment and improved living standards for our people.

From the work of pioneers in quality and productivity measurement and improvement methods, and the experience of many firms and organizations throughout the world, we know how to do it. Applying the 16 Points described in this book can make productivity improvement happen.

UNDERSTANDING THE 16 POINTS

The 16 Points are best presented as interconnected elements in a circle, or globe, representing the expanse of the organization. For strong and steady productivity improvement these 16 Points must work together to drive performance everywhere. Figure 2 shows the

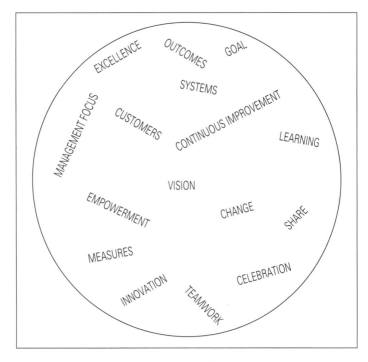

Figure 2. The 16 Points Embedded in the Culture of the Organization

interconnection and mutual support of the 16 Points. Each relates to and supports the others; all are embedded in the culture of the organization. All together they make productivity improvement happen.

1

VISION

Create a Vision and structure operations to make it happen.

Vision answers important questions:

- What is success?

- What matters most? There are so many options. So many products, services, markets, customers, prospects. So many concepts. So many methods.

- What is our future?

Success, continuing success, and constant and continuing improvement has to be created in many steps, by many people, at many levels. Big steps may transform the organization, with the work of transformation and the benefits widely shared. Smaller steps will be taken at all levels, shared among the people at those levels. The driving theme at all levels however, is that the players share a common purpose. Vision is the starting point.

Vision provides focus, direction, motivation, and a community of interest and aspiration. It says, for everyone in the company, *"This is what we're all about."* Out of all that's possible, Vision says where we're going. It sets a direction into the future.

A Vision is a short statement of the company's drive and direction. It's the essence of the company's competitive advantage, to be created and grown. All company members participate in making it happen, and benefit from the results. Some Visions:

N.A.S.A. Put a man on the moon by the end of the decade.

Henry Ford. Produce a car that everyone can buy.

Disneyland. Create a place for people to find happiness and knowledge.

Girl Scouts. Help a girl reach her highest potential.

McCaw Cellular Communications. Provide an automatic call delivery system that connects people to people, not to places.

Baxter Healthcare Corporation. Be the leading single source of products and services which help hospitals to achieve cost-effective, high-quality health care.

With a company Vision as a starting point, units within the company can create Visions that drive their performance. Examples:

Automotive and Miniature Lighting Division. Sustain a leadership position by providing the highest quality light sources and lighting systems at competitive prices.

Plastics Division. Be the market leader by excelling in product quality, new technology, and service to customers.

A Vision that works to create a realistic, credible, attractive future belongs not only to executive leadership, but to the whole organization—to everyone. It's a guiding light—a star to steer by. Leadership creates a Vision that is right for the organization, sets the direction toward that Vision, and leads the organization through the changes needed to get there.

The right Vision for the organization

- fits the organization and the times

- sets a standard of excellence

- clarifies direction and purpose

- inspires enthusiasm and commitment

- is clear and easy to understand

- evokes the unique strengths of the organization to create competitive advantage

- is ambitious

Once created, the Company Vision becomes its banner, a symbol that sets direction for the future. The Vision Statement needs to be seen everywhere, all the time. It must be in company publications and on plaques and displays. On bulletin boards, in management reports, and in stockholder reports, and financial statements. In project proposals and requests for expenditure. In budgets and plans, in policy manuals, and included in work standards. It must be in all the places that company members see every day in the work they do, and in all the places that other company constituencies see in their contacts with the company. The Vision must be everywhere. Everywhere that words appear, there also appears the Company Vision. On signs. On paper. On computer screens. On PA systems and e-mail. Everywhere. And unit Visions the same, within the unit.

Vision paints a picture of the future. The next step for all members of the company is a clear view of "*what the Vision means for me*." We all need to know, accept, and support our part in realizing the Vision. This can be done by setting specific goals, feedback measures, and action plans everywhere that work is done — all focused on the Vision.

2

GOAL

Make improving Total Productivity a key goal of
management at all levels.

WHAT IS PRODUCTIVITY?

Productivity is the engine of improvement. Every work station contributes to productivity. Every work group is a productive unit. Each productive unit needs to measure its productivity and set goals to improve that measure.

Productivity is the ratio of the defect-free output(s) of a given group to the input used to make or provide those outputs (whether products or services):

$$\text{Productivity} = \frac{\text{Defect-Free Output}}{\text{Input}}$$

MEASURING PRODUCTIVITY

In some work units, labor (or perhaps labor and materials) may be the only relevant input(s). Their single output is clear and tangible. Then productivity can be tons or units of that product per worker or tons per worker-hour.

Higher levels of the organization have more complex outputs that the company often measures in dollars rather than physical counts. Inputs now include all business costs:

labor, materials, energy, capital, and anything else used. Thus *total productivity* can be expressed as:

$$\frac{\$ \text{ Output}}{\$ \text{ Labor} + \$ \text{ Materials} + \$ \text{ Energy} + \$ \text{ Capital} + \$ \text{ Other}}$$

or

$$\text{Total Factor Productivity} = \frac{\$ \text{ Value added}}{\$ \text{ Labor} + \$ \text{ Capital}}$$

where $\$$ = constant dollars.

Value added represents $\$$ *Sales* less *purchased goods and services (materials, energy, and other)*. It is of interest to organizations with major materials or upstream business services purchases.

As processes are improved and waste eliminated, the ratio improves. Improvements in quality increase the numerator and/or decrease the denominator in the total productivity formula. Productivity and quality come together as a management strategy. Workers see how they contribute.

TRACKING PRODUCTIVITY MEASURES

Tracking total productivity and total factor productivity measures over time provides senior executives an early warning sign of profitability change. Measured in current dollars, the trend of these measures adds the discipline of the market to the improvement efforts and demonstrates the organization's basic health.

But further studies of these measures is needed. Changes in the total measures may come from a short-term product mix shift or from a highly-focused waste reduction program. One is fleeting and the other is permanent. Further diagnosis of productivity measures at all levels is what most of the organization works with and acts upon for local improvement.

3

CUSTOMERS

Focus productivity improvement on creating customers
and satisfying their expectations.

CREATING AND KEEPING CUSTOMERS

The success of a company depends on creating and keeping customers:

- with products, services, and pricing that satisfy customer expectations

- at costs that provide profitability to the company

Productivity performance makes it possible both to satisfy customer expectations and establish the cost structure that provides profitability for the company.

With the right products and services to deliver, productivity in marketing, sales, and service delivery creates customers and delivers satisfaction. Productivity throughout operations makes this market performance possible by providing the needed outputs and costs.

Everything focuses on the customer, beginning with the products and services needed to satisfy customer expectations. (See Figure 3.) By producing and delivering those products and services, the company receives from customers:

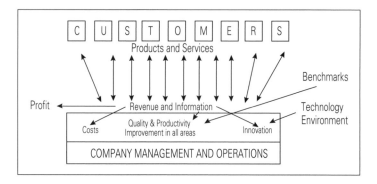

Figure 3. Customer Focus

- revenue
- information/feedback

Revenue pays all costs and provides targeted profitability, *if* the company has been productive in its work. Information and feedback help the company:

- continuously improve productivity and quality in all areas
- innovate new products, services, and methods

Innovation for change and improvement also comes from outside benchmarks and technology sources.

The SME Wheel

The Society of Manufacturing Engineers (SME) emphasizes how manufacturing can focus on a customer-oriented Mission and Vision to strive for continuous improvement. In the SME "Manufacturing Enterprise Wheel," everything centers on the customer. (See Figure 4.)

Reengineer for Customer Focus

A plastics products company had been losing money for three years. They decided to reengineer their operations

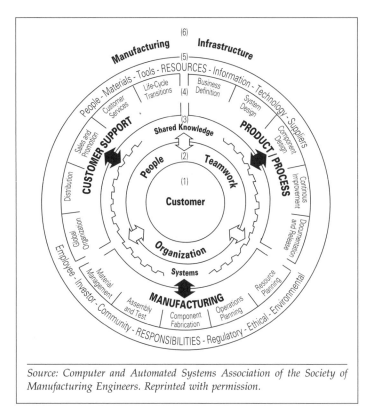

Source: Computer and Automated Systems Association of the Society of Manufacturing Engineers. Reprinted with permission.

Figure 4. Manufacturing Enterprise Wheel

beginning with a sharp focus on customers and markets. (See Figure 5.) They analyzed product/market segments and customers and identified problems and opportunities. Based on this information they established new goals and performance measures.

The primary responsibility of marketing and sales is to create and keep customers. All other functions perform to make this happen as well. The company therefore established new goals and performance measures for these

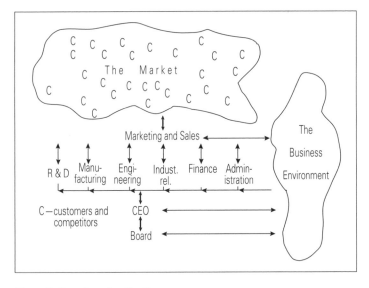

Figure 5. Reengineering the Company

functions, too. They also changed their organizational structure and processes to make the new performance possible. Within a year the company was profitable and their success continues.

CUSTOMERS AND EMPLOYEES

For everyone in the company, customers and prospects are the focus for the work they do. Some employees produce final outputs for the company's customers. Others produce intermediate outputs for internal customers, whose needs and expectations also must be satisfied.

Every function of every enterprise produces and delivers outputs to customers. By actively seeking information from customers and from the business environment, a company can set goals at all levels and measure performance. Feedback measures help people do their jobs and continuously improve. The organization chart turns upside down—customers are at the top. Everyone in the company acts to

- create customers
- satisfy customer expectations

Productivity goals and measures make it happen.

4

OUTCOMES

Include in productivity measures the long-term outcomes
of all company actions.

Total Productivity includes in output measures only defect-free products and services produced, delivered to customers, and satisfying customer expectations. This is the customer view of output. It's not the company count. It's the customers' count that matters.

In measuring and monitoring productivity trends we need to take into account not only product and service output, but also longer-term outcomes and their consequences:

- What outcomes result from company products and services over their life cycles?

- What are the longer-term outcomes of other company actions?

If a company years later must clean up toxic waste, the remediation is an outcome. Product liability and other litigation are outcomes. The costs of writing off unsold products and unneeded capital equipment, and losses on business units that are sold or shut down — these are outcomes too. Restructuring that results from inattention to changing conditions can be a costly outcome. New applications and new markets for a company's technical

Plus	**Minus**
New uses for company products and technology	Remediation of environmental contamination
Recycling of company output as a business opportunity	Cost of recycling company output
New business resulting from investment in company R & D	Losses on business units that are sold
Gains on business units that are sold	Customer claims
	Product liability
	OSHA, EEOC, and other litigation
	Costs of writing off unsold products and unneeded capital equipment

Figure 6. Outcomes

innovation are outcomes, too — on the plus side. Figure 6 lists some representative outcomes.

Those affected by such longer-term outcomes are our customers, too.

The following formula is a customer-focused measure of Total Productivity:

$$\text{Total Productivity} = \frac{\text{Defect-free, Customer-satisfying output}}{\text{Inputs of: Labor}}$$

Capital
Materials
Energy
Other purchases

For a measure of long-term productivity, including consideration of outcomes as well as outputs, use the following formula:

$$\text{Long-term Productivity} = \frac{\text{Life cycle revenue (LCR)}}{\text{Life cycle costs (LCC)}}$$

LCR: Total revenue from sales of products and services over the life-cycle time frame (constant $)

LCC: Costs of inputs plus costs of outcomes over the life-cycle time frame (constant $)

Note: The calculation in current $ can also be a useful measure.

This long-term productivity measure can be used for the entire company, and for profit center businesses in the company.

For practical use of the long-term productivity formula, select a time period that covers the output/in-use experience/after-use consequences/other outcomes time frame. Calculate the measures and monitor trend, and take actions as appropriate.

A good way to start is to calculate the measurement for the past year or two (if data are available) and for the current year. Continue the measurement annually, monitoring trend and implementing actions as appropriate. From experience, seek to improve the measurement method and the use of the measures in decision making.

Future outcomes are difficult to perceive from the vantage point of today. That's partly because we haven't been looking for them. But we can use a customer measure of output to measure current productivity performance. And we can measure current outcomes from past outputs and actions. Taking these measures and making them a part of our management information system can help us improve both outputs and outcomes. Scanning ahead for likely outcomes from current actions becomes part of the decision process. Both current and long-term productivity improves.

5

MEASURES

*Have everyone develop specific performance measures
and related goals.*

Every group in the organization needs a set or family
of measures:

- to help define and clarify their role
- to prioritize their actions

Groups choose their family of measures based on the strategic priorities that reach them from higher in the organization and from direct and indirect customer feedback. But the workers themselves should choose the specific measures. People work better towards measures they help select.

Workers who "do" the work at each level can develop measures that are:

- very understandable
- controllable by the work they do

The family of measures might include one or two from each of several categories. A total of four to six measures ensures proper focus.

Alternative categories are:

- "pure" productivity (O/L, O/K, O/M)
- internal quality (waste, yield, defects)

- customer satisfaction (surveys, rejects)
- timeliness (on-time, cycle time)
- safety (accidents, reportables)
- housekeeping/environment
- documentation (accuracy, on-time)
- utilization of fixed resources
- team effectiveness
- innovation/creativity
- marketplace activity

These measures should make up part of a structured (but informal-looking) feedback system. Local workers — those doing the work — are first to get the data. They discuss the data among themselves and take initial corrective action.

At higher levels in the organization, and in parts of the organization close to the final customer, measures heavily reflect total output. Elsewhere measures more often reflect intermediate outputs, costs, and times.

Examples of families of measures are:

Work Group

- output/hour
- defect rate in process
- certifications/employee
- unplanned scrap
- on-time delivery

Profit Center/Company

- total productivity
- total factor productivity

- market share index

- new products/total products

- quality awards and citations

- environmental index

The internal measures that relate to cost are much more useful in improvement work if they adopt the principles of activity-based costing. This attaches the costs to the reason they were incurred ("driver") rather than by useless designation of their nature followed by nearly arbitrary allocation to labor-hours or square footage.

If the organization can develop measures that successfully balance local understanding and motivation with headquarter's strategic focus, the organization will have the maximum alignment and effectiveness in its competitive tasks.

6

EMPOWERMENT

Empower people. Put responsibility and authority
where the work is done.

The work of an organization and its parts derives from its mission, its structure, and its strategic plan. The organization is in place for a customer-related reason. Breaking down the customers' needs into required activities and steps gives form to the organization. It marshals resources and contributes to a strategic plan to do what needs to be done in each time period to satisfy that customer need. If the organization communicates all this clearly, the members are then ready to think about *how* the work is to be done.

One way to get work done is to give orders downward. If all the above has not been clearly communicated, it may be the only way to get things done. If subordinates do not understand the mission and customer-driven plan, taking orders is all they are prepared to do. But successful organizations rely on the people who do the work at each level to make their own decisions and act at that level. They provide resources and support to accomplish the task. This is called empowerment.

Empowerment is a management style in which work responsibility is assigned and explicitly accepted. Both the assigner and the assignee accept a set of principles of behavior. There is joint responsibility for:

- defining the boundaries of the work
- identifying the resources needed
- agreeing on the goals; what is completion and success.

The assigner:

- accepts responsibility to clearly define the work
- provides the necessary resources (such as training, tools, and support)
- is available to review or otherwise help as the work is done
- avoids intervening in the details of the work and methods unless asked
- recognizes and rewards success

The assignee:

- puts together the work plan
- reports progress
- controls costs
- solicits help as and if needed

In its simplest form, empowerment can be found in the day-to-day relationship between leaders and immediate subordinates. But the more powerful forms of empowerment require removing the many layers and barriers in a traditional organization. If the top manager identifies a problem, the people who are directly involved many layers down gather to solve the problem. The "hand-off" is relatively informal and prompt. This is the power in empowerment!

Alternatively, the work group itself may identify the problem. In either case, the problem is resolved. Control of the empowerment process does not come from day-to-day surveillance and intervention by higher-level management. Control comes from the organization's shared Vision, and the supporting Mission, goals, and measures that guide decisions and actions at each level. Everyone does what they do best. All of us are smarter than any of us. The capabilities of empowered people have no limits!

7

TEAMWORK

Teamwork works! Develop teams at all levels.

Empowerment and teams tend to be found together in normal practice. Respect for the ability of individuals at any level to solve problems is at the root of empowerment. This respect for individual ability directly leads to the recognition that combining the abilities of several of these individuals brings all the more chance of solving problems well.

Individuals, however brilliant and motivated, have inherent limitations. They only have 24 hours a day. They can only lift so much. They are occasionally sick. But beyond physical limitations, individuals have only their own direct experience to draw on. Complex problems need solutions that converge from many directions to solve all aspects of the problem. It takes a combination of experiences and capabilities to solve complex problems. *It takes teams*!

Most organizations have two kinds of teams:

- temporary, or special-purpose, teams
- permanent, routine teams

The temporary teams work to solve one particular problem or type of problem and then they disband. They exist outside the standard organization chart. They are "parallel structures" that do not get in the way of regular work. They may be very important. Examples are labor-management cooperation teams that deal with outside-bargaining issues in large plants. Benchmarking teams make a profound study of a key business process. When the members are working on these teams they are not doing their "real jobs."

The permanent operating team is on the organization chart. This is their "real job." But the exact nature of an individual's job may change frequently. These teams can be highly structured, carrying out the minute-to-minute will of a "boss." But more typically they are at least partly self-managed. On some (or all) issues they make their own decisions, heavily based on customer feedback, and allocate their own resources and efforts.

Self-managed teams tend to exhibit several special characteristics derived from the empowerment relationship:

- They usually strive for maximum interchangeability among members (to hedge against absenteeism and to broaden the experience of each and all).

- Their communication is fanatically clear; they may appear to pay more attention than is necessary to make sure everyone understands everything.

- They seek, rather than resist, new methods and tools; frequently they are the first to suggest changes.

- They tend to be highly customer-oriented, whether the customer is external or internal to the organization.

- They pay close attention to schedules and cycle-times, since they have full responsibility in that area.

- They tend to provide frequent and innovative recognition to members.

Teamwork, as a concept, rises above the structure of the organization. An employee can be a good team member even in a situation where most employees work on an individual basis. This is due to executive style and tradition or because of inherent characteristics of the work. Both football teams and skiing teams are "teams," but they are very different. Football is highly interactive work. Each player is interdependent with the others on the field. Even those on the bench influence the efforts of those in the field. Short pieces of heroic individual action occur, but planned action centers on collective maneuvers and tactics. Skiing, on the other hand, is only individual heroic action. The other teammates support and advise, but there is no collective action.

Groups, working as teams, can produce better end results working on jobs than can groups whose members work as individuals. But every team member, when doing their part of the collective activity, still has to exhibit individual excellence for the team to succeed. The goal is to further extend individual capability through teamwork!

8

CONTINUOUS IMPROVEMENT

Continuously improve work processes. Find and eliminate waste. Simplify and standardize. Use visual controls and mistake-proofing devices.

CONTINUOUSLY IMPROVE PROCESSES

Improve work processes! That's the focus of Total Productivity improvement, as it is also the focus of Total Quality Management. One of the pioneers in developing this concept was Allan Mogensen. Working more than half a century ago, he called his methods "Work Simplification," and outlined them in these steps:

- Chart work flow
- Analyze work flow
  - ➤ Eliminate the unessential
  - ➤ Simplify the essential
- Develop new work flow proposal
- Make users owners
- Install new work flow
- Monitor results
- Involve all concerned in the process

Over recent years, Total Quality Management experience has developed an extensive resource base on the reengineering of business and work processes. These methods produce more and better results, using fewer resources. And they work at all levels, from production processes on the plant floor to business processes in the executive suite.

Here are basic steps for managing processes to control and improve performance:

1. Define the process.

2. Establish ownership.

3. Establish process boundaries and interfaces.

4. Flowchart the process, identifying:

   ➤ value adding stages

   ➤ control points

   ➤ waste.

5. Implement measures of process performance.

6. Observe comparable processes inside or outside the organization to find better solutions already in place.

7. Take corrective actions as needed.

8. Use the process measures to continually improve performance.

9. Involve those doing the work in all the above.

Figure 7 shows a checklist to use for auditing the management of work processes.

Process:_____ Owner:_____
Team Members:

	Rating	
Process Requirements	Acceptable	Unacceptable
1. Process is specified, with control points	_____	_____
2. Boundaries and interfaces are defined	_____	_____
3. Process has an owner	_____	_____
4. A work team is responsible for process output	_____	_____
5. Customer(s) clearly identified, needs known and included in work standards	_____	_____
6. Work output and quality are defined and measured	_____	_____
7. Feedback measures are used by those doing the work, for process control and improvement	_____	_____
8. Similar processes elsewhere have been observed and analyzed	_____	_____
9. Cycle time is measured	_____	_____
10. Value Added and Non-Value Added time is measured	_____	_____
11. Visual controls and mistake-proof devices (poka yoke) are used at control points	_____	_____
12. Customer satisfaction/dissatisfaction is known	_____	_____
13. A corrective action system identifies error and waste and takes corrective action	_____	_____
14. Recognition is received for good performance	_____	_____

Figure 7. Process Management Checklist

FIND AND ELIMINATE WASTE

The major opportunity for improving work processes lies in finding and eliminating waste. A useful definition is:

Waste is anything that adds cost without adding value.

Using a value added measure improves processes. It finds waste, shortens cycles, reduces cost, and improves quality. It changes and broadens our whole concept of waste. The Japanese describe seven classes of waste:

- waste in processing
- inventory
- over-production
- waiting
- transport
- unnecessary motion
- defects

Most waste is invisible. So the task is, first of all, to find waste. It's often hard to see. Here are same examples of waste:

Visible:

- out-of-specification incoming material
- scrap (raw materials, WIP, finished goods)
- downtime
- rework (blue collar)

Often **invisible:**

- rework (white collar, professional, management)
- resources used to produce out-of-specification or unnecessary output

- setups, clean-outs
- queue time, work-in-process
- wait time (people, machines)
- inventory (raw materials, WIP, finished goods)
- moving work-in-process from one place to another
- over-production
- engineering changes
- unnecessary reports
- non-value adding business travel
- meetings that don't efficiently produce a value-adding result
- management processes that take too long, revise too many submissions too often, involve too many people doing — and redoing — too much work

Charting process steps and classifying them as "value adding" or "non-value adding" will find a lot of unseen waste. Timing the steps, and reducing and eliminating this waste can often shorten cycle times 50 to 80 percent. Time can be a powerful metric for improvement!

Managing work processes requires work standards for all points where work is done. Here are some useful methods for developing work standards:

- Relate standards to customer requirements.
- Involve employees in developing the standards.
- Understand the performance of similar work inside and outside the organization, and appraise differences.
- Use all five senses in specifying work standards.
- Use computer-assisted instruction.

- Cross-train employees in working to the standards.

- Use automated equipment at work stations, such as manufacturing and assembly automation, CRT screens, automated inspection.

- Use visual controls, such as photographs, samples, video.

- Use mistake-proofing devices (poka-yoke).

- Use color codes.

- Develop work standard sheets, and work instruction forms.

Support work standards with visual controls and mistake-proofing devices at value adding stages and at supplier/customer interfaces (both internal and external).

9

EXCELLENCE

Find best practices. Benchmark key business processes.

Set goals to equal or exceed. Strive for excellence.

BENCHMARKING AND IMPROVEMENT

Alert organizations improve everything continuously. But resources are limited. Where should we apply the improvement effort first? The simple answer: where improvement is most needed. But where is that? There is plenty of uncertainty about:

- the actual level of current performance

- whether performance is "good enough" relative to what is necessary in the coming competitive situation.

Benchmarking can provide answers. Benchmarking systematically compares elements of performance in an organization against those of other organizations. Usually the aim is mutual improvement. Comparisons can be in many different places, using varying means and different collaborators. They all arrive at the same thing: *an understanding of where the organization is now, so realistic goals can be set and resources intelligently applied to get the most important improvements per unit of effort.*

Most important improvements reflect both competitive urgency and size of the problem. Sometimes a relatively small problem in dollars may be the critical problem. Similarly "effort" could have either key people's time or dollars as the determining factor as to what to study first.

Strategic Benchmarking

Strategic benchmarking uses industry comparisons to get "macro" information on how the organization might be importantly different in major functions such as

- research and development
- manufacturing
- marketing
- globalization
- maintenance
- training
- other key areas where strategic choices can be made

Typically, trade associations or industry-specialist consultants sponsor such studies. Survey questions cover intensity, type, and nature of the strategic variables.

Strategic benchmarking may lead to business process benchmarking. Process benchmarks can best be done with firms outside of the industry with a single or small group of benchmarking partners. Base your selection on the following criteria:

- customer/supplier relationships
- geographical proximity
- executive ties
- business magazine fame
- consultant's recommendation

Partners share information in the search for best practices for all. Note that true "best" practices:

- have to be carefully defined as to what kind of "best" (cost, product specs, quality, timeliness, etc.)

- are often found in not-so-famous organizations who happen to specialize in that certain area

Consensus Benchmarking

As shown in Figure 8 a consensus model of process benchmarking technique includes:

- careful identification of the process to be studied

- development of a representative study team (including people from the process under study)

- creative search in the public domain and private sources for leads about what "best" looks like and who has it

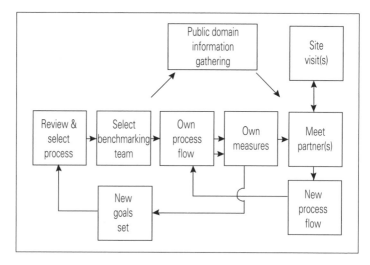

Figure 8. Process Benchmarking

- parallel flowcharting of the company's own processes to bring transparency to often secret procedures and habits

- identification (or development if necessary) of performance measures for the process

- meeting with partners to critique approaches and create new alternatives

- site visitation to see other alternatives in action

- installation of agreed-upon new approach in each organization

- establishment of appropriate goals for the new approach (not necessarily stopping at "equaling" the partner's or a competitor's performance)

BENCHMARKING AND GOAL-SETTING

Benchmarking is valuable to any organization to improve goal-setting and to make breakthrough improvements. Less recognized is its value as an organizational development tool. Not only do team members benefit, everyone can see the benefit of systematic study that involves people from all parts of the work force.

10

INNOVATION

Innovate! Encourage creativity. Search for and adopt new technology. Change and improve products, processes, information systems, communications, organization structure, and methods.

Business success depends on constant and continuing improvement in everything the company is now doing. On-going success also requires finding and using the right new technologies and methods in company products, services, and ways of working. Continuously improve the old. Continuously innovate the new and better. Both productivity and innovation are essential.

Constant and continuing improvement involves everyone finding and implementing ideas for improving performance in their areas of work. Throughout the company improvements by the hundreds and thousands combine for steady improvement of overall company performance. Separate from, or in addition to, ongoing company operations, groups also work on innovations. New technology, new concepts, new ways of working can make big change happen fast. Breakthrough change. Innovations. Companies can tap the ability of all their people to do things better. They can also organize to encourage and support creativity and innovation, to

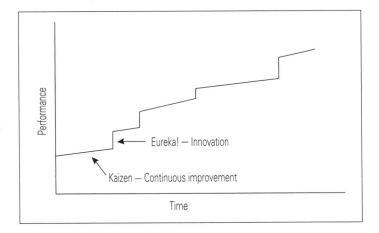

Figure 9. Kaizen/Eureka!

do things differently. They can combine the power of continuous improvement (Kaizen) with the power of innovation (Eureka!) Kaizen/Eureka! Figure 9 illustrates the power of this combination.

In the midst of revolutionary technological change, the company must find the new technology it needs to create its intended future — its Vision. The new technologies will be software and humanware as well as hardware. They will be organizational as well as product and process. The new technologies may come from internal research and development. More likely, they will be found in outside sources. In all areas, there is always a better way. Creativity will find it. Innovation will make it happen.

Innovation is different from ongoing operations. It's not a fallout from standard operating procedures. It's a different nature and needs a different nurture. Successful companies organize for innovation and support creativity and innovation by inspiring the formation of Innovation Projects. Such projects typically form at the corporate and unit headquarters levels. They can form at any level where

Innovation Projects:
1. Make significant change happen:
   - New technology
   - Major new product
   - Major new service
   - New process
   - New business venture
2. Are defined in terms of the customer
   - Who are the customers?
   - What are customer needs, values?
   - What unique benefits will be offered?
3. Have a specific goal to be achieved by a target date
4. Have project boundaries and relationships with other company units clearly defined
5. Have an agreed-upon structure supported by an authorized budget
6. Are led by a Project Champion committed to making the project succeed
7. Use project management methods that are separate and different from the management of on-going operations. Some characteristics:
   - Project Plan, comprising:
     - ➤ Task assignments. For each:
       - o scheduled start/end dates (as of plan date)
       - o results expected
       - o responsibility assignment
       - o performance measure
     - ➤ Milestone reviews
       - o expected deliverables
       - o project decision gates:
         - – go
         - – go, with changes
         - – no-go
   - Project Management Style
     - ➤ Self-managed teams
     - ➤ Informal, qualitative
     - ➤ Heuristic – learning the way
     - ➤ Fast-acting. Do it! Fix it!
       - o Barriers? Go over, under, around, through. Keep going.
       - o Problems? Resolve.
       - o Opportunities? Exploit.

Figure 10. Innovation Projects

change is needed. Figure 10 summarizes the characteristics of successful Innovation Projects.

Projects develop people as they develop the company. In their work, project team members experience all business functions — planning, research, engineering, manufacturing, marketing, finance, personnel, logistics, and legal. All these skills combine to match technology to opportunity and make innovation happen.

Innovative companies set goals and performance measures for innovation. And each innovation includes goals and measures for continuing improvement. Innovation + Productivity. Ongoing cycles of change and continuous improvement.

11

MANAGEMENT FOCUS

Create a work structure that produces the desired results.

Support people.

How you structure work determines the work that is done, how it's done, and the unit's operating results. The structure of work in a management unit includes:

- statement of purpose — Vision — what the unit is and does to accomplish a desired result.
- resources:
    - ➤ people
    - ➤ capital
    - ➤ materials
    - ➤ energy
    - ➤ information
- performance measures
    - ➤ at process check points
    - ➤ at work stations
    - ➤ of end results:
        - ○ Productivity
        - ○ Quality

- ○ Output

- ○ Profit or profit contribution

- ○ Training, development, participation

- ○ Environmental relationships

- information flow

Managers manage people. That's obvious. But if the obvious were always the reality, a flat earth would have foiled the discovery voyage of Columbus! Things are not always as they seem.

About every twenty years or so an important new discovery is made: People can manage themselves! Self-management can increase group capability dramatically. It's simple arithmetic. All of us are smarter than any of us, and can do much more. Managers become coaches rather than commanders; facilitators rather than controllers. Managers become leaders, focusing on goals and creating a structure of work that can produce the desired results. Self-management can then produce the results. Every member is a manager.

Self-management works effectively when the work is structured to produce the desired results. The management focus is on the work processes. Manage these processes. Support the people working the process to produce the outputs that will satisfy their customers' expectations, without error, without waste.

To achieve desired results, leaders focus on the following:

1. Meaningful goals that everyone understands and accepts

2. Work processes that are capable of producing the desired results

3. Necessary process inputs

4. Qualified process team members

5. Feedback performance measures that help team members do their jobs

6. Recognition

When leadership provides this environment, self-management produces outstanding performance.

12

LEARNING

Create a learning organization. Make ongoing education and enriching work experience part of every job.

Many organizations have "learning disabilities." The people involved may be capable of mental growth, especially if the organization practices an empowerment ethic. But group disability may arise from:

- insufficient attention to the details of education and training

- an insufficiently broad concept of how and where learning takes place

Both *experience* and *learning events* need more attention. Learning comes mostly from the everyday workplace through everything the employee (and leader) does. If empowerment is presented as an opportunity to be proactive in improving everything in sight, the main prerequisite is in place for a learning organization.

Experience can be truly misleading as a measure of learning. Twenty-five years of experience doing a wide variety of responsible things can make an exceedingly valuable employee. Twenty-five iterations of the same year of experience is worth less than a single run-through of that year. Little was gained and flexibility was totally lost.

An organization's education and training efforts can be valuable if they follow a few easy-to-state (but not necessarily easy-to-follow) rules:

- Separate "extend/stretch" training from "upgrade/ salvage" training or everyone will be only a step above salvage.

- Balance training offerings and individual curricula between managerial, behavioral, and technical subject matter.

- Use internal trainers and "cascading" (leaders train employees) where it works. Use external trainers where it does not work—no room for ideology here.

- Do most detail training on-the-job by or with the immediate supervisor.

- Acknowledge that training is a form of empowerment, a shared responsibility between supervisor (guide course selection and follow-up later on the job) and learner (seriously try to use the new tools on the job).

- Measure training. Outcome measures (can they use the tool a few months later?) are much more valuable than activity measures or exit polling.

- Use "pop-quizzes" as post-training expectation. Mastery is important.

- Cross-train your trainers and consultants in addition to your employees; myopia occurs everywhere.

- Acknowledge that education and training are work; just like regular work is work. Do not let the "fun imperative" get in the way of the need to learn.

The road to a "learning organization" starts with structured events. But as the organization matures, more of the learning takes place informally and voluntarily. The best steering mechanism for the organization is the example the people at the top set. As empowerment becomes real, learning becomes real. Major improvements from fundamental, quantum shifts in approach become more likely. Learning-driven success breeds more learning.

13

SYSTEMS

*Use system thinking and system models to aid decisions
at all levels.*

....

The typical organization chart shows people, functions, and units, and where they fit in the company hierarchy. It shows little about how the organization actually works.

A system model also shows functions and units, but in a very different way. This model includes the information system, communication channels, markets and customers, the external environment, and the interconnectivity among all of these. The model shows how the system works.

Organizations can develop a system model for the total company system, and for each of the various function and unit subsystems. They can use such models to reengineer structure and to audit and redesign information systems. This can provide the information needed at all levels for control and continuous improvement of work processes.

Figure 11 shows a system model for a corporate division with four profit center businesses. The model shown is the Viable System Model that Stafford Beer developed, as applied in a division of a large corporation.

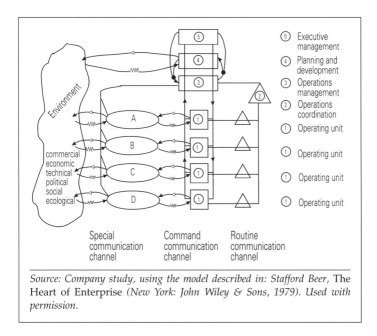

Source: Company study, using the model described in: Stafford Beer, The Heart of Enterprise *(New York: John Wiley & Sons, 1979). Used with permission.*

Figure 11. System Model for a Corporate Division

Similar models were developed for each of the four profit center operating units as well. Each model shows:

• executive and functional management

• operating units

• information channels

• information flow

• environmental links

One company, while working out a Vision/Mission/Total Quality road to its future, redrew its organization chart as a system model. As Figure 12 shows, the new model is not composed of lines and boxes. And, it shows

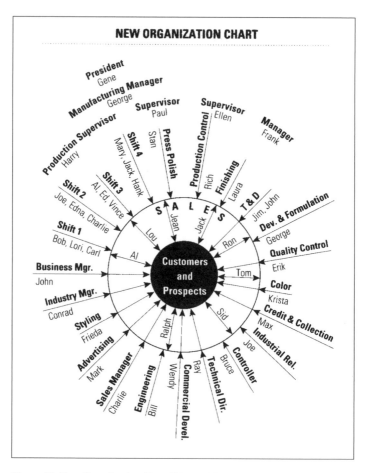

Figure 12. New Organization Chart (Circle of Communication and Teamwork)

customers and prospects as the focus for everything the company does.

All functions support sales, and collaborate through the Circle of Communication and Teamwork. Many company people in addition to the sales staff interact with customers to deliver satisfaction. The "focus lines" on the chart show these contacts. Some go to customers. Others go only as far as the Circle of Communication and Teamwork. The president supports all functions and interacts with customers. Creating and keeping customers has become the focus of all company actions.

With this point of view and this purpose, the company has created a high-performance organization that turned a record of losses into a new record of high profitability.

14

CELEBRATION

Recognize, celebrate, and reward productivity improvement.

Even with the very best improvement efforts, the question arises: "What's in it for me?" There are many answers. A focus on productivity through empowerment leads to a much more interesting workplace. It extends personal development. It provides opportunities—a bigger playing field with bigger issues. And it may provide raises and promotions.

RECOGNITION

World-class organizations do more than this, however. They delight their employees, just as they delight their customers and shareholders through extra value. Public recognition of excellent performance is now common with many organizations. Here are some examples:

- articles in magazines

- lunches

- plaques

- events for individual high-performers

- all-hands celebrations for an entire group

Public recognition is a step beyond a pat on the back. But, many will still feel that this is not the kind of reward they deserve.

Part of the problem is who does the recognizing. Recognition from an esteemed leader is valued highly by the recipient. But the rest of the work force may feel it lost that round; that politics dictated the award rather than intrinsic merit. On the other hand, if the employees themselves give the awards, they preserve fairness, but the recipient may be somewhat underwhelmed. The motivation and feelings of responsibility of the work force will be enhanced by:

- prompt rewards

- rewards proportional to the accomplishment

- selection with input from both executives and employees

REWARD

Beyond these various light recognition schemes is the pay-for-performance philosophy: individual and group incentive plans. Companies have long used these at the executive level. Not surprisingly, executives support them as a way of stimulating extra effort and providing executives a stake in the company. Somehow, those same executives may oppose this reasoning when it comes to the rest of the work force. They are already well-paid. They do not have sufficient influence on the fortunes of the company to qualify for such incentives.

INCENTIVES

Some of the most progressive companies have found ways to provide incentives for both individual workers and the work group. Individual plans center around obtaining additional skill certifications. These can be professional certification or simply internal certifications for other tasks within the team or work cell. Welders might go to night school and become certified as electricians. Personnel clerks might become accountants or lawyers on their own. The carton filler may learn how to run the machine from which the carton contents flow. At first these horizon-expanders may be of additional value only for vacation relief. But eventually the company is saved the difficulty of locating and orienting a new electrician, lawyer, or machine operator (and the trouble of laying-off a welder, personnel clerk, or carton filler). Where the company pays horizon-expanders additional monies just because they have the additional capability, regardless of whether they are actually serving at that moment in the new role is collectively called pay-for-knowledge. Contrary to practice in professional baseball, the utility player may be paid more than the starter, at least if the starter is not in a critical position.

At the group level, there are several approaches to incentives through bonus payment. Profit sharing is best known. All employees receive a part of corporate profits beyond a certain target, which may or may not have been predetermined. This pool of profit is spread to employees based on their base pay or some other "fair" criterion. These profit sharing plans are popular with senior executives because they are easy to understand and explain. The work force naturally finds them better than nothing. But, usually companies pay profit sharing on a deferred and/or retirement basis. And they sometimes pay in company stock, which employees may or may not perceive as a worthwhile reward.

The best-received group incentive plan from the work force's point-of-view is gainsharing. Here the payout pool is based on one or more measures that the local work force has control over. The payout is immediate (same month or quarter or, at worst, same year). And it is normally in cash. Gainsharing plans are usually linked to empowerment philosophies and team structures. Local employees usually are involved in designing the plan and help administer it once it is launched. Gainsharing generates positive motivation and even a certain amount of group discipline with the work force itself motivating the slackers.

Key steps in developing an effective gainsharing plan include:

- definition of boundaries and participation rules
- development of a communication plan by the design team
- selection of appropriate measures and agreement on their dollar value
- agreement on frequency, share, and split
- baseline adjustment conventions
- linkages with involvement efforts, individual appraisal, and company profit picture

Gainsharing provides the best possible linkage of rewards to strategic plans, performance measures, and identified improvements. Gainsharing organizations successfully "put their money where their mouth is," and the regular employees can join their senior executives in having a stake in the company's success.

15

SHARING

Share your experience. Help government and community organizations improve productivity too.

....

Organizations cannot be separated from the communities in which they are located. Products and services cannot be sold into extreme instability. A framework of law (and habit) is necessary. The community's education system prepares people for work in the organization. Employees continue to live in the community as they work. Their health and well-being is maintained by the hospital and medical structure. They are protected by the community's environmental restrictions. They participate in religious groups.

Thus there is nothing special about an organization supporting its communities. They pay taxes! But there is a big difference between the minimum legal level of support and proactive support. Proactive support is mostly through people's time and intelligence. Intellectual contributions are the most leveraged of all, because they are a scarcer resource than money.

Some of the contributions from an organization may be one-shot help. Teaching a government to bid out a service they had been doing themselves only needs to be taught in one bidding cycle. After that it becomes routine. Bringing in a new industry may only happen once, but the new industry provides accelerated growth of contribution by its unique additions to the community. Providing new pieces of science equipment for the schools or the teaching of quality techniques are leveraged. Do it once and the recipients will spread it on. Organizations can create contests or loan training materials year after year. Even unleveraged help is still help.

Many communities in the United States have adopted total quality principles and are starting to reform (reinvent) their local services and interrelationships. This sort of cooperation was always potentially available, but it is hard to separate political issues from improvement. The successful local governments are distinguishing the *what* from the *how*, not unlike separating the physical from the financial. It is up to the local governments to come up with the *what* by traditional political means. But the volunteers can do a completely nonpartisan job of advising *how* a government can best do the indicated task, based on how private industry has done it.

Community implies a fifty-mile radius, but other relevant, larger communities are the nation and the world. Assisting the Federal government to accomplish a task at lower cost and/or higher quality ultimately benefits the whole nation, including those who have voluntarily helped. Most businesses, even if they feel their relationship with the Federal government is a net negative, at least benefit if government initiatives can be done more quickly and at lower cost than before.

In this age of competitive trading blocs, it is hard to talk about international cooperation. But other nations will not buy goods and services of the United States unless:

- the goods and services meet their specifications as customers, transcending cultural and traditional boundaries
- they have something that can and will be sold in return.

The former is just good business, extending good domestic practice internationally. The latter depends on political "playing fields," but it can be enhanced by a good job of the former — meeting customer needs no matter what it takes.

16

CHANGE

Embrace change! Use these 16 Points and keep improving!

Everyone wants success. And we want success for our company, our government, and our community, too. Improving productivity is an important part of that success. Change toward better and better results is change we can embrace. Productivity improvement inspires us with energy, and rewards us with organization success, personal satisfactions, and rising income.

Productivity change is exciting work. The 16 Points in this book outline how to do it. They are a road map to success in the first task of management. Improve productivity! Following the road map:

- causes change

- helps us respond to the change around us

But change is not the goal. Productivity improvement is the goal. Change just happens. These 16 Points can ensure that change is improvement; change to something better. Fact-driven change to ongoing success. A wealth of experience is compounded into these 16 Points. They work.

When we improve productivity there is more to share, with more opportunity still ahead. And, in organizations in which productivity improvement thrives, with their flatter structures and empowered people, everyone shares in the benefits and the opportunities. Constant and continuing improvement. Constant and continuing success. Constant and continuing personal growth.

ABOUT THE AUTHORS

William F. Christopher is president of The Management Innovations Group. Previously he worked in sales, marketing, R&D, executive, and consulting positions in Hooker Chemical, Occidental Petroleum, and General Electric. He has worked with more than one hundred businesses in seventeen countries.

Christopher is the author of three books on business management, and coeditor of *The Service Quality Handbook*, the *Handbook for Productivity Measurement and Improvement*. He is editor-in-chief of the *Management Master Series.*

William F. Christopher, The Management Innovations Group, P.O. Box 8240, Stamford CT 06905.

Carl G. Thor is president of Jarrett Thor International. Previously he served as president and vice chairman of the American Productivity & Quality Center, responsible for the Center's work in productivity measurement and gainsharing. Earlier positions were with Anderson Clayton and Humble Oil. He has led industry studies and statistical research projects, conducted workshops, authored articles, and is contributing author and coeditor of the *Handbook for Productivity Measurement and Improvement.*

Carl G. Thor, Jarrett Thor International, 771 Battery Place, Alexandria, VA 22314.

The Management Master Series

The *Management Master Series* offers business managers leading-edge information on the best contemporary management practices. Written by highly respected authorities, each short "briefcase book" addresses a specific topic in a concise, to-the-point presentation, using both text and illustrations. These are ideal books for busy managers who want to get the whole message quickly.

Set 1 — Great Management Ideas

1. *Management Alert: Don't Reform—Transform!*

   Michael J. Kami

   Transform your corporation: adapt faster, be more productive, perform better.

2. *Vision, Mission, Total Quality: Leadership Tools for Turbulent Times*

   William F. Christopher

   Build your vision and mission to achieve world class goals.

3. *The Power of Strategic Partnering*

   Eberhard E. Scheuing

   Take advantage of the strengths in your customer-supplier chain.

4. *New Performance Measures*

   Brian H. Maskell

   Measure service, quality, and flexibility with methods that address your customers' needs.

5. *Motivating Superior Performance*

   Saul W. Gellerman

   Use these key factors—nonmonetary as well as monetary—to improve employee performance.

6. *Doing and Rewarding: Inside a High-Performance Organization*
   Carl G. Thor

   Design systems to reward superior performance and encourage productivity.

PRODUCTIVITY PRESS, Dept. BK, PO Box 13390, Portland, OR 97213-0390
Phone (503) 235-0600   Fax (503) 235-0909

Set 2 — Total Quality

7. *The 16-Point Strategy for Productivity and Total Quality*
   William F. Christopher and Carl G. Thor
   Essential points you need to know to improve the performance of your organization.

8. *The TQM Paradigm: Key Ideas That Make It Work*
   Derm Barrett
   Get a firm grasp of the world-changing ideas behind the Total Quality movement.

9. *Process Management: A Systems Approach to Total Quality*
   Eugene H. Melan
   Learn how a business process orientation will clarify and streamline your organization's capabilities.

10. *Practical Benchmarking for Mutual Improvement*
    Carl G. Thor
    Discover a down-to-earth approach to benchmarking and building useful partnerships for quality.

11. *Mistake-Proofing: Designing Errors Out*
    Richard B. Chase and Douglas M. Stewart
    Learn how to eliminate errors and defects at the source with inexpensive poka-yoke devices and staff creativity.

12. *Communicating, Training, and Developing for Quality Performance*

    Saul W. Gellerman
    Gain quick expertise in communication and employee development basics.

These books are sold in sets. Each set is $85.00 plus $5.00 shipping and handling. Future sets will cover such topics as Customer Service, Leadership, and Innovation. For complete details, call 800-394-6868 or fax 800-394-6286.

PRODUCTIVITY PRESS, Dept. BK, PO Box 13390, Portland, OR 97213-0390
Phone (503) 235-0600   Fax (503) 235-0909

BOOKS FROM PRODUCTIVITY PRESS

Productivity Press provides individuals and companies with materials they need to achieve excellence in quality, productivity, and the creative involvement of all employees. Through sets of learning tools and techniques, Productivity supports continuous improvement as a vision, and as a strategy. Many of our leading-edge products are direct source materials translated into English for the first time from industrial leaders around the world. Call toll-free 1-800-394-6868 for our free catalog.

Handbook for Productivity Measurement and Improvement
William F. Christopher and Carl G. Thor, eds.
An unparalleled resource! In over 100 chapters, nearly 80 front-runners in the quality movement reveal the evolving theory and specific practices of world-class organizations. Spanning a wide variety of industries and business sectors, they discuss quality and productivity in manufacturing, service industries, profit centers, administration, nonprofit and government institutions, health care and education. Contributors include Robert C. Camp, Peter F. Drucker, Jay W. Forrester, Joseph M. Juran, Robert S. Kaplan, John W. Kendrick, Yasuhiro Monden, and Lester C. Thurow. Comprehensive in scope and organized for easy reference, this compendium belongs in every company and academic institution concerned with business and industrial viability.
ISBN 1-56327-007-2 / 1344 pages / $90.00 / Order HPM-B242

A New American TQM
Four Practical Revolutions in Management
Shoji Shiba, Alan Graham, and David Walden
For TQM to succeed in America, you need to create an American-style "learning organization" with the full commitment and understanding of senior managers and executives. Written expressly for this audience, *A New American TQM* offers a comprehensive and detailed explanation of TQM and how to implement it, based on courses taught at MIT's Sloan School of Management and the Center for Quality Management, a consortium of American companies. Full of case studies and amply illustrated, the book examines major quality tools and how they are being used by the most progressive American companies today.
ISBN 1-56327-032-3 / 606 pages / $50.00 / Order NATQM-B242

PRODUCTIVITY PRESS, Dept. BK, PO Box 13390, Portland, OR 97213-0390
Phone (503) 235-0600   Fax (503) 235-0909

The Unshackled Organization
Facing the Challenge of Unpredictability Through
Spontaneous Reorganization

Jeffrey Goldstein

Managers should not necessarily try to solve all the internal problems within their organizations; intervention may help in the short term, but in the long run may inhibit true problem-solving change from taking place. And change is the real goal. Through change comes real hope for improvement. Goldstein explores how change happens within an organization using some of the most leading-edge scientific and social theories about change and reveals that only through "self organization" can natural, lasting change occur. This book is a pragmatic guide for managers, executives, consultants, and other change agents.
ISBN 1-56327-048-X / 208 pages / $25.00 / Order UO-B242

20 Keys to Workplace Improvement

Iwao Kobayashi

This easy-to-read introduction to the "20 keys" system presents an integrated approach to assessing and improving your company's competitive level. The book focuses on systematic improvement through five levels of achievement in such primary areas as industrial housekeeping, small group activities, quick changeover techniques, equipment maintenance, and computerization. A scoring guide is included, along with information to help plan a strategy for your company's world class improvement effort.
ISBN 1-915299-61-5 / 252 pages / $45.00 / Order 20KEYS-B242

TO ORDER: Write, phone, or fax Productivity Press, Dept. BK, P.O. Box 13390, Portland, OR 97213-0390, phone 1-800-394-6868, fax 1-800-394-6286. Send check or charge to your credit card (American Express, Visa, MasterCard accepted).

U.S. ORDERS: Add $5 shipping for first book, $2 each additional for UPS surface delivery. We offer attractive quantity discounts for bulk purchases of individual titles; call for more information.

INTERNATIONAL ORDERS: Write, phone, or fax for quote and indicate shipping method desired. For international callers, telephone number is 503-235-0600 and fax number is 503-235-0909. Prepayment in U.S. dollars must accompany your order (checks must be drawn on U.S. banks). When quote is returned with payment, your order will be shipped promptly by the method requested.

NOTE: Prices are in U.S. dollars and are subject to change without notice.

PRODUCTIVITY PRESS, Dept. BK, PO Box 13390, Portland, OR 97213-0390
Phone (503) 235-0600   Fax (503) 235-0909

NOTES